#VETTECHLIFE

Coloring

Coloring

Coloring

Coloring

Coloring

Coloring

Coloring

Coloring

Coloring

Coloring

Coloring

Coloring

Coloring

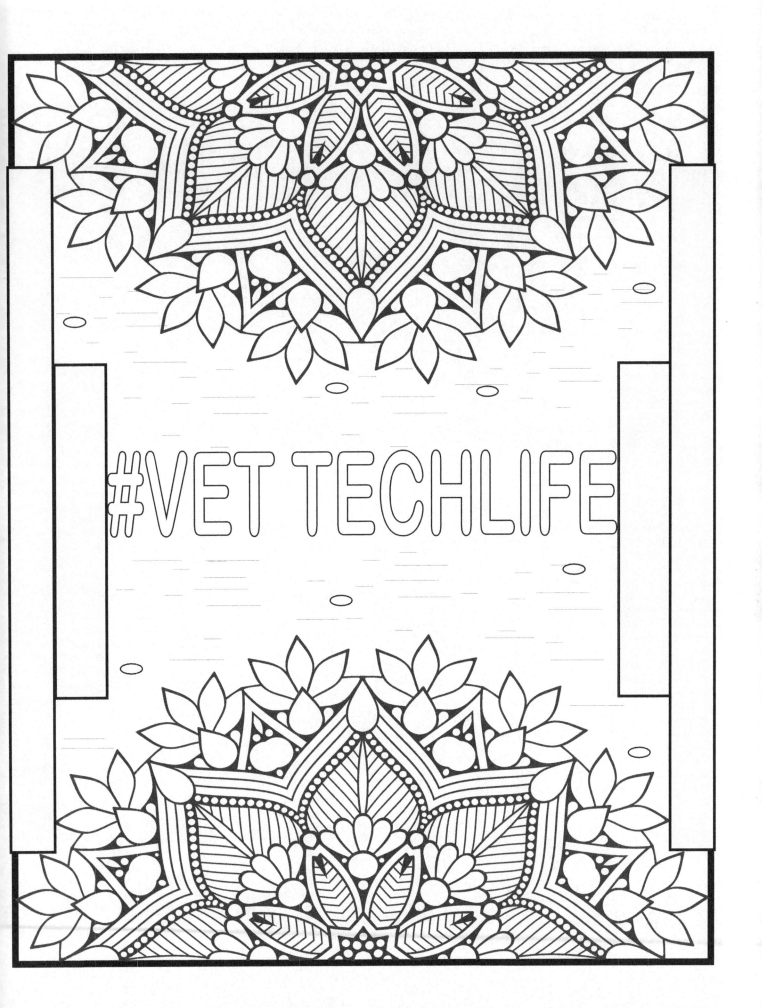

Coloring

Coloring

Coloring

Coloring

Coloring

VET TECH
Because
Freaking
Miracle
Worker
Is not an official
Job
Title

Coloring

Coloring

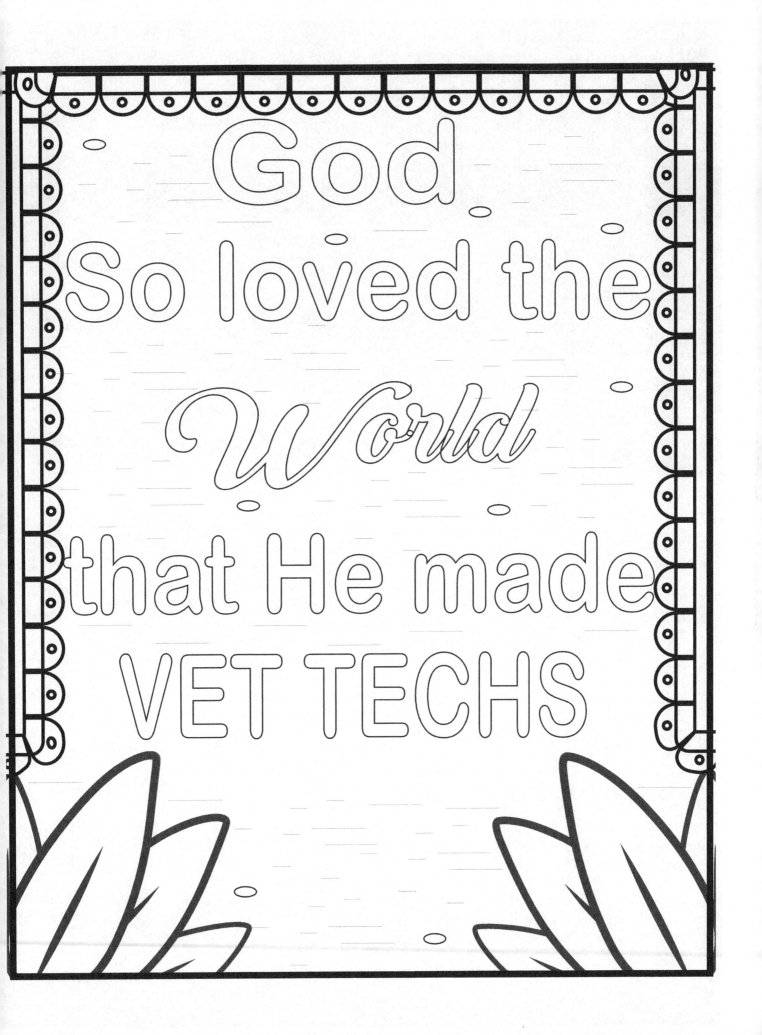

Coloring

Coloring

Coloring

BE A
VET TECH
THEY SAID

IT WILL BE
Fun

THEY SAID

Coloring

Coloring

Coloring